FLIGHT

BALLOONS, KITES, AIRSHIPS AND GLIDERS

June Loves

This edition first published in 2002 in the United States of America by Chelsea House
Publishers, a subsidiary of Haights Cross Communications

Chelsea House Publishers
1974 Sproul Road, Suite 400
Broomall, PA 19008-0914

The Chelsea House world wide web address is www.chelseahouse.com

Library of Congress Cataloging-in-Publication Data Applied for.
ISBN 0-7910-6563-4

First Published in 2000 by
Macmillan Education Australia Pty Ltd
627 Chapel Street, South Yarra, Australia, 3141

Text copyright © June Loves 2000

Edited by Lara Whitehead
Text design by if Design
Cover design by if Design
Page layout by if Design/Raul Diche
Illustrations by Lorenzo Lucia
Printed in Hong Kong

Acknowledgements

The author and the publisher are grateful to the following for permission to reproduce
copyright material:

Cover: hot air balloon (center), courtesy of Global Ballooning ; inflating hot air balloon
(background), courtesy of Great Southern Stock.

Photographs courtesy of: Australian Picture Library/John Carnemolla, p. 17 (bottom);
Australian Picture Library/Corbis-Bettmann, pp. 4, 5, 9, 12-3; Australian Picture Library/
David McClenagahan, pp. 3 (right), 29; Australian Picture Library/Oliver Strewe, p. 19;
Australian Picture Library/Vandystadt, pp. 2 (right), 25 (top); Blackwood Picture Library,
pp. 20–1; Coo-ee Historical Picture Library, pp. 10–1, 14–5, 23 (bottom); Global Ballooning,
pp. 6–7; Great Southern Stock, pp. 2–3 (background), 8, 24–5, 30–1, 32; International
Photographic Library, pp. 11 (top), 15 (right); Lochman Transparencies/Len Stewart, p. 16;
The Photo Library/Peter J. Robinson, p. 27 (top); Sporting Images/Darryl Peroni, pp. 22–3,
/Andrew Shield, p. 21 (bottom right); Ruth Lathlean/World Images, p. 28.

While every care has been taken to trace and acknowledge copyright the publishers
tender their apologies for any accidental infringement where copyright has proved
untraceable.

Contents

Early balloons

BALLOONS HAVE PLAYED an important part in the development of flight. For hundreds of years, people dreamed of flying with wings. A few people tried to fly by launching themselves from cliffs and buildings with bird-like wings strapped on. However, flapping mechanical wings proved to be unsuccessful. Instead, the first people to fly used the simple scientific knowledge that hot air rises.

THE MONTGOLFIER BALLOON

In the 1700s, the French brothers Joseph and Etienne Montgolfier designed the first successful flying craft, a hot-air balloon.

The first balloon passengers were a sheep, a duck and a rooster. They made a short flight on September 19, 1783. The Montgolfier brothers sent the animals up in the balloon to make sure it was safe for people to travel this way.

On November 21, 1783, the Montgolfier balloon took to the skies with people. The balloon was filled with hot air warmed by a fire underneath. As it floated over Paris for 12 kilometers (7.5 miles), it was the first flight to carry humans.

The Montgolfier balloon was made of cloth and paper and was beautifully decorated.

HYDROGEN-GAS BALLOONS

On December 1, 1783, two Frenchmen, Jacques Charles and Nicholas Robert, made the first free flight in a balloon filled with **hydrogen** gas. In two hours it flew 43 kilometers (26.7 miles), which was longer and further than the Montgolfier hot-air balloon had done only ten days earlier.

Within two years of these early balloon flights, people were using hot-air and hydrogen-gas balloons to cross the English Channel.

Ballooning in the nineteenth century

Gas ballooning became a popular society sport in the nineteenth century. People enjoyed this new and thrilling sport and they began to compete for distance and height records. At leisure resorts, people could take sight-seeing flights over the countryside.

An engraving drawn in the 1700s of a balloon being filled with hydrogen gas in Paris. Hydrogen gas was produced by pouring sulfuric acid upon filings of iron.

5

Parts of a hot-air balloon

A HOT-AIR BALLOON is a huge envelope, or bag, made of light material that is filled with heated air. Passengers are carried in a basket or gondola suspended underneath. Hot-air balloons rise because the air inside the bag is warmer (and lighter) than the surrounding air.

The envelope is made of tough, but light, nylon. The bigger the envelope, the more weight it can lift into the air

The skirt channels hot air into the envelope

The rigging wires hold the basket to the balloon envelope

Propane gas is burned in the gas burner to keep the air in the envelope hot

The basket is made of light, flexible wicker and holds the crew, gas cylinders and the flight instruments

Short ropes hold the basket

VH-AFP

HOW HOT-AIR BALLOONS WORK

Air that has been heated by the hot flames of a gas burner rises and collects in the balloon.

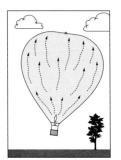

1 When the air inside the balloon is hot, it gives enough lift to overcome the balloon's weight. The balloon rises from the ground and soars into the sky.

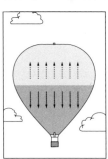

2 As it rises, the hot air in the balloon begins to cool and the lift gets weaker. When the lift equals the balloon's weight, the balloon stops rising and floats at the same height in the air.

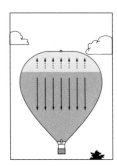

3 As the hot air cools further, the lift becomes less than the balloon's weight. The balloon begins to sink.

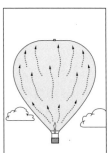

4 To keep the balloon flying, the pilot turns the burner on again. Short bursts of flame keep the air inside hot. The lift stays strong enough to keep the balloon from sinking.

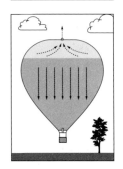

5 To descend, a valve at the top of the balloon opens to release the hot air. Cold air replaces the hot air. The balloon becomes heavier and is able to descend and land.

 Flying Fact

The height of the hot-air balloon depends on how hot the air is inside the envelope.

Modern balloons

MODERN HOT-AIR BALLOONS are used for leisure and sport. They are very large and can carry people in the basket beneath the envelope. Light, yet tough, synthetic material is used for the envelope. Separate panels of material are cut to a pattern and many different shapes are made. They are airtight, fireproof and rip-proof.

Ballooning is an exciting and popular sport all over the world today. People take part in rallies and races to break long-distance records.

Helium balloons

Helium balloons are filled with helium gas rather than hot air. Helium is lighter than air and does not need to be heated in order to lift the balloon. These balloons can fly much higher than hot-air balloons.

PROBLEMS FOR HOT-AIR BALLOONS

✴ There is no control over the direction of a hot-air balloon. The direction of the flight depends on where the wind takes the balloon. You can wait a long time for the wind to be in the right direction. You could go in the wrong direction when the wind changes.

✴ Bad weather conditions make it difficult to travel in a hot-air balloon.

✴ Balloons can only carry a small number of passengers.

Inflating a hot-air balloon.

Early airships

INVENTORS KEPT EXPERIMENTING with better ways to travel in the air. They began adding power to control balloons so they could be steered from one destination to another.

In 1852, a Frenchman named Henry Giffard built the first airship. It had a cigar-shaped balloon filled with coal gas and was powered by a light steam engine linked to a **propeller**. It travelled through the air at eight kilometers (five miles) per hour for 2.7 kilometers (1.7 miles).

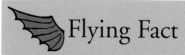

Flying Fact

Airships were also known as 'dirigibles'. The word comes from Latin and means 'steerable'.

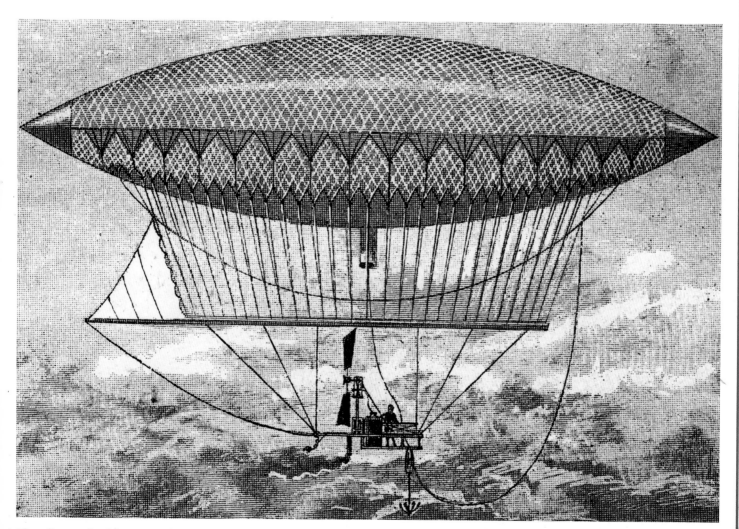

The first airship was built by Henry Giffard in 1852. It could only be steered in calm weather.

Parts of an airship

AIRSHIPS ARE CRAFT that are lighter than air. They are self-propelled and are steered. Like balloons, airships float because of their gas-filled envelope. A cabin, or gondola, underneath is used to carry passengers. Engine-driven propellers move the airship through the sky. Horizontal and vertical **rudders** are used to steer the airship.

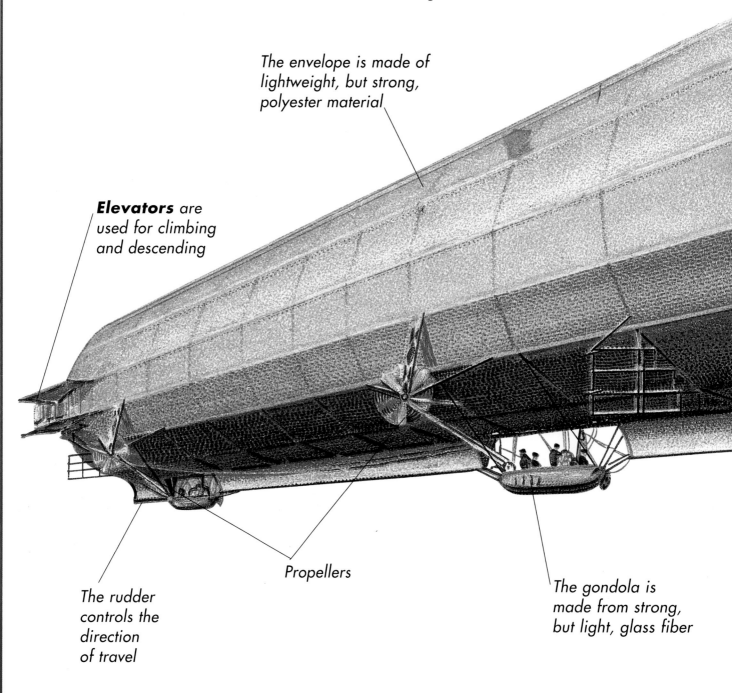

The envelope is made of lightweight, but strong, polyester material

Elevators *are used for climbing and descending*

The rudder controls the direction of travel

Propellers

The gondola is made from strong, but light, glass fiber

Blimps are non-rigid airships. They are often used for commercial purposes.

TYPES OF AIRSHIPS

Early airships had a floppy cloth envelope filled with hydrogen. Passengers travelled in a cabin hanging underneath.

As airships became bigger, the envelopes were stiffened for support. Medium-sized airships had **struts** fitted to their envelope to stiffen them.

There are different types of airships.

Rigid airships or 'Zeppelins' are built with a solid framework to keep their shape. Bags to hold the gas are held within the solid shape.

Non-rigid airships are known as 'blimps'. They have a series of strong bags joined together with no frame. They become cigar-shaped when filled with gas.

Semi-rigid airships use a combination of framework and gas to make their shape.

The ballonet is an internal bag that traps air. There are two.

Ballonet valve. Air is pumped into or out of the ballonets to alter the weight of the airship.

11

The great airships

THE FIRST SUCCESSFUL rigid airship was the LZ-1, which was built by the German Count Zeppelin in 1900. By 1910, the German Airship Transport Company had regular services between German cities. Before World War I broke out, 35 000 passengers were carried by these airships.

During World War I, airships were adapted for military **reconnaissance** and bombing. Airships were used to make many raids but they were easily attacked. After the war, pioneering work continued on airships in many countries. However, the lighter-than-air hydrogen gas in their bags caught fire easily. This caused a number of horrific fires and crashes.

Airships used to have propellers turned by large diesel engines. The propellers were mounted on **pylons** to keep them clear of the gas bags.

The Graf Zeppelin 11's four diesel engines produced about 1,000 horsepower each. Its maximum speed was about 130 kilometers (80.8 miles) per hour.

Flying Fact

The great airships were called Zeppelins after Count Ferdinand Zeppelin, the German general who invented them.

HOW AIRSHIPS FLY

Airships have engine-driven propellers and can be steered in any direction. Moving the rudder and elevators tilts or turns the airship as it flies through the air. To make the airship go up or down, gas or air can be pumped in or out of the air-tight ballonets.

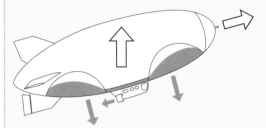

When air is pumped out of the ballonets, the airship is light enough for the helium gas in the envelope to lift it up into the sky.

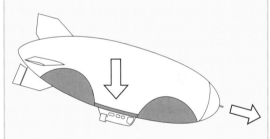

To make the airship heavier and bring it down, air is pumped into the ballonets by the engines.

GRAF ZEPPELIN

THE HINDENBERG DISASTER

The Hindenberg was the pride of the Zeppelin Airline. It was the largest rigid airship ever built and was about 245 meters (803.8 feet) long. It used flammable hydrogen gas.

The Hindenberg was designed to carry about 100 passengers and 45 crew in a regular passenger service between the United States and Europe. It was very luxurious and had two-berth cabins, a viewing cabin, dining room, lounge and smoking room.

The Hindenberg was launched in 1936 but crashed in flames a year later. Thirty-six of the 97 passengers were killed.

THE GREAT AIRSHIP ERA ENDS

People did not want to travel in airships after the Hindenberg disaster. Although thousands of passengers had travelled in airships since 1910, airships were no longer seen to be a safe means of travelling.

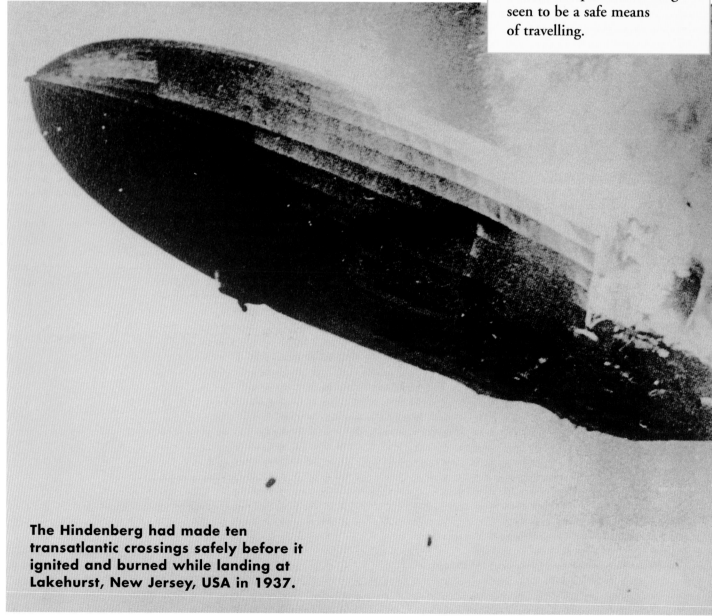

The Hindenberg had made ten transatlantic crossings safely before it ignited and burned while landing at Lakehurst, New Jersey, USA in 1937.

MODERN AIRSHIPS

Modern airship designs have improved as new materials have been developed, new gases made and new engines invented. They are made of materials such as carbon-fiber and plastic **composites**. Helium gas, which does not burn, is used instead of hydrogen.

The pilot of a modern airship steers by moving fins on the tail. Passengers and crew travel in comfort in the cabin suspended underneath.

Today, airships are used for aerial photography and filming, advertising and military surveillance, as well as performing rescue missions and early warning duties. One of the advantages of airships is they can stop in mid-air without using valuable fuel.

THE FUTURE OF AIRSHIPS

In the future airships may prove an effective and successful way of transporting passengers and heavy **cargo** over long distances. Many new projects are being explored for the future commercial use of airships.

Kites

KITES ARE ANCIENT flying machines. They have been made in all sorts of shapes and sizes, and for many different purposes. Early kites were not designed as toys. They were used for cultural and religious ceremonies and sometimes for military purposes. Photographs were taken from kites during the Spanish-American War and kites were used for ground-to-air gunnery practice during World War II. Today, kites are used for many purposes. In Antarctica they are used for weather forecasting. They carry instruments such as barometers, thermometers, and wind gauges to record the weather.

THE FIRST KITES

The first kites were made in China over 3,000 years ago. Early kites were made of expensive silk and bamboo and only the rich could afford them. When paper was invented, kites became more affordable and very popular.

Modern kites are made in many different shapes and sizes.

TYPES OF KITES

Box kites

Laurence Hargrave invented the first box kite in 1893. Hargraves's type of kite played an important part in the invention of the airplane because the Wright brothers later used box kites to develop their airplane's wings.

A box kite is complicated to make. A combination of triangle, square and rectangle shapes can be used to make box kites. They are more stable and have better lift than a diamond-shaped kite.

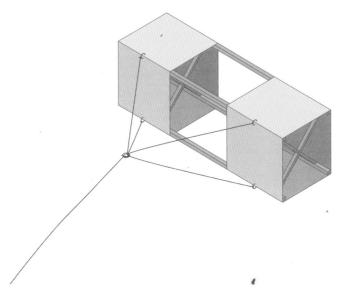

A simple box kite made of two open-ended boxes.

Kites at the Festival of the Winds, Sydney, Australia.

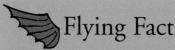 Flying Fact

In 1752, Benjamin Franklin, the famous US scientist, flew a kite during a thunderstorm to prove that lightning was actually electricity. The experiment was successful, but he was very lucky he was not killed.

Human-carrying kites

Many early inventers believed that huge human-carrying kites had a future as flying machines. Alexander Bell, the inventor of the telephone, invented a kite that lifted a US Army officer to a height of over 50 meters (164 feet).

Recreational kites

Kite flying is a popular hobby and sport all over the world. Kite flying as a sport is challenging and exciting. Just like any sport, it takes a great deal of practice to become a champion kite flier in competitions.

The high-performance kites used in competitions are made from special materials. They are scientifically designed to perform in particular ways and in certain weather conditions. Some kites have two strings, others have four.

How kites fly

KITES DEPEND ON wind to fly. They fly because they are held in the air by the force of the wind pushing against them. The wind rushing over the top of the kite goes faster than the wind flowing underneath it. This difference in air flow creates an upward lifting force on the kite.

Kites fly best in a good breeze. A kite's weight is very small in comparison to the strength of the forces of lift and **drag**. Some kites can fly in a very gentle breeze if they are light and their surfaces are wide. The wide surfaces give the breeze a large area from which to produce lift.

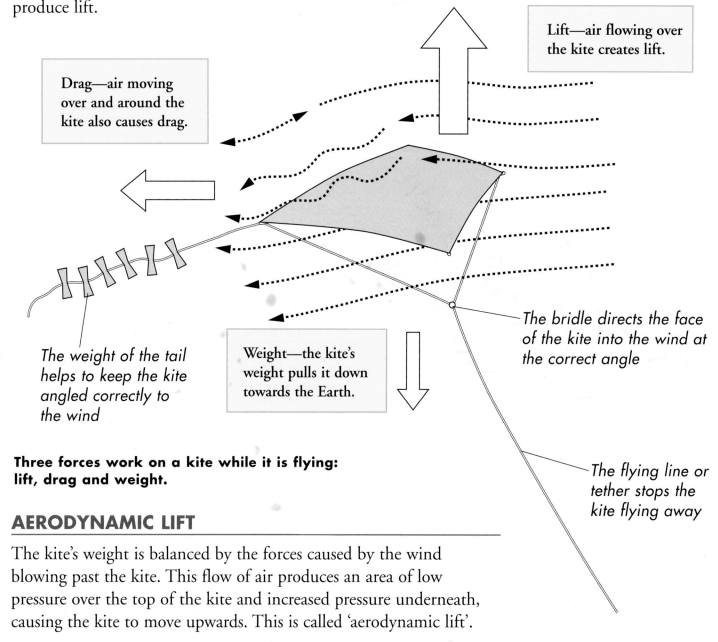

Lift—air flowing over the kite creates lift.

Drag—air moving over and around the kite also causes drag.

The weight of the tail helps to keep the kite angled correctly to the wind

Weight—the kite's weight pulls it down towards the Earth.

The bridle directs the face of the kite into the wind at the correct angle

The flying line or tether stops the kite flying away

Three forces work on a kite while it is flying: lift, drag and weight.

AERODYNAMIC LIFT

The kite's weight is balanced by the forces caused by the wind blowing past the kite. This flow of air produces an area of low pressure over the top of the kite and increased pressure underneath, causing the kite to move upwards. This is called 'aerodynamic lift'.

A complex box kite.

MANEUVERABILITY

A flat, diamond-shaped kite flown by a single string is the most common kite. Its shape is one of the oldest and simplest of kite designs. The tail and the way the control string is attached to the kite are important to keep the kite flying at the correct angle to the wind.

Greater maneuverability can be obtained when two lines are attached to a diamond-shaped kite. If one line is pulled more than the other, one side of the kite comes down and the other side lifts, causing it to turn. Pulling the left line causes it to turn to the left, pulling the right line causes it to turn to the right.

Hang-gliders

A hang-glider is shaped like a giant kite. Most of them are **delta** shaped with a frame made of aluminum and covered with nylon. The pilot is held underneath the frame in a harness. The hang-glider flies by gliding on air currents. The frame is strong, light and portable. It is easy to fold, carry and reassemble.

Flying Fact

Some hang-gliders use a flight bag instead of a harness for support and to keep them warm.

HANG-GLIDER DESIGN

The main canopy of a hang-glider was designed by American Professor Francis Rogallo in 1950. He designed a steerable parachute for bringing equipment from space back to Earth. It had a delta-shaped wing made from fabric. People began to fly Rogallo wings by hanging beneath them and shifting their body weight to steer.

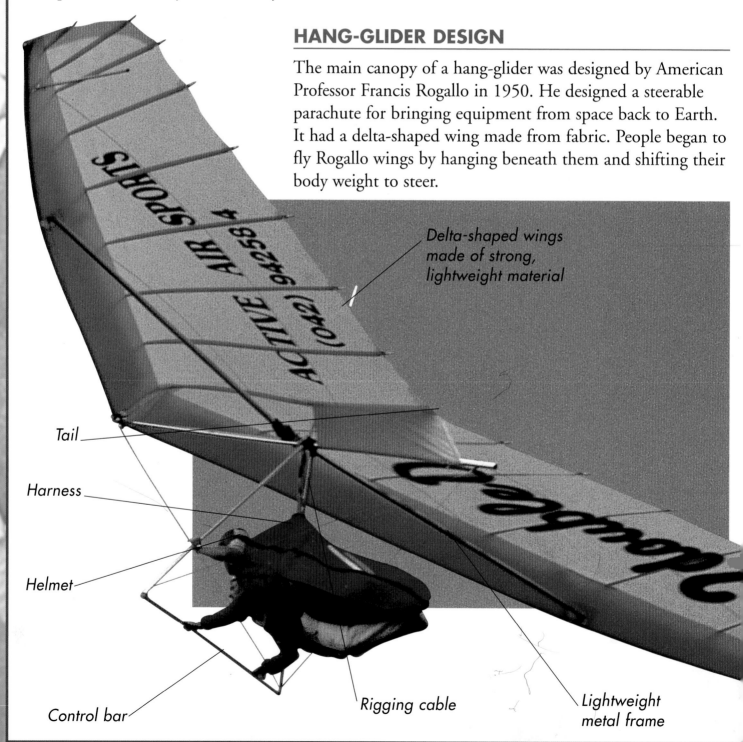

Delta-shaped wings made of strong, lightweight material

Tail

Harness

Helmet

Control bar

Rigging cable

Lightweight metal frame

HOW TO FLY HANG-GLIDER

Hang-glider pilots take off by jumping from the top of cliffs, hills or mountains. The hang-gliders spiral upwards in **thermals** of air to gain height.

A hang-glider is steered by the control bar. Moving this bar changes the position of the pilot's body weight and the angle of the wings. Pushing the control bar out makes the hang-glider go up.

Like **gliders** and winged aircraft, a hang-glider will only fly if it is moving fast enough to keep air flowing smoothly past its wings, creating lift. Rising air currents help to keep the hang-glider in the air.

A clear sunny day is best for hang-gliding. Thermals are strongest on a clear day when the sun can warm the ground. When the air above the ground warms, it floats upwards and forms a thermal.

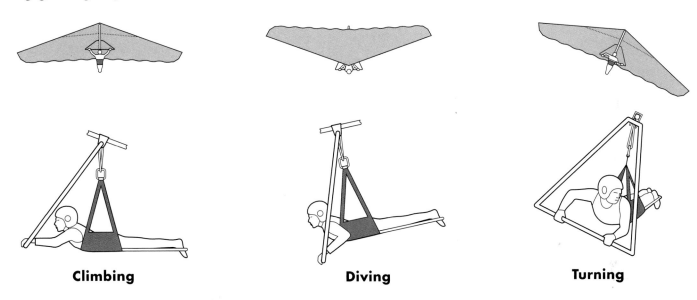

Climbing   **Diving**   **Turning**

Hang-gliders often take off by running off the edge of a cliff or down a steep hill.

Gliders

A GLIDER IS AN AIRCRAFT that does not have an engine. It uses currents of warm, rising air to help it glide in the sky. Gliders have long wings that provide plenty of lift. Because gliders do not have an engine, they can only fly if they are towed into the air.

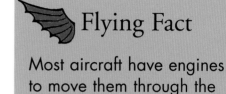

Flying Fact

Most aircraft have engines to move them through the air. Air flows over the wings, giving the aircraft lift, which helps it stay in the air.

A glider in flight.

A glider in flight.

GLIDING BIRDS

Some birds can glide in the air for very long distances. They glide with their wings stretched flat and still. Albatrosses, with their long narrow wings, can glide over the ocean for hours.

EARLY GLIDERS

After hot-air balloons and airships were invented, people used them for air travel. However, people still dreamt of flying with wings like the birds. Inventors kept finding ways to fly in the air using wings.

Sir George Cayley

Sir George Cayley (1773-1857) was an English inventor who believed that by using wings people would be able to fly. Cayley experimented with kites to find ideas for his designs. One of Sir George Cayley's designs was for a triplane, a three-winged glider. At the back was a tail to keep the glider flying straight during its flight.

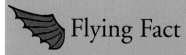

Flying Fact

The Wright brothers built, tested and flew different gliders before they designed the first airplane.

Otto Lilienthal

Otto Lilienthal (1848-96) was a German engineer who built several gliders. He flew them as he hung underneath the wing. Lilienthal controlled the gliders by shifting his weight. Lilienthal was killed after he crashed one of his gliders.

Octave Chanute

Octave Chanute (1832-1910) was another famous early inventor of gliders. Chanute and his team built and flew many gliders. They were made of wood with wire frames covered by thin material.

Otto Lilienthal flying his glider.

How gliders fly

Gliders, hang-gliders and birds use thermals to gain height during flight. Because they are lightweight, they gain height when circling in thermals.

STAYING UP

A glider will only fly if it is moving fast enough to keep air flowing smoothly past its wings to create lift. Gliders gradually descend back to the ground unless they are flying in air that is rising at a rate faster than the glider's normal rate of descent.

HOW THERMALS ARE MADE

Thermals occur when a column of warm air rises from heated parts of the ground. Air also rises when the wind meets rising ground such as hillsides, mountain ranges and coastal sand dunes.

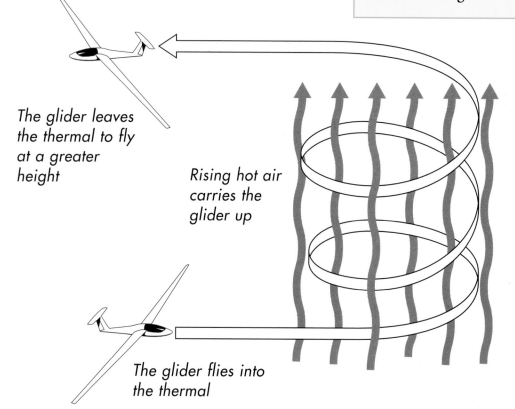

The glider leaves the thermal to fly at a greater height

Rising hot air carries the glider up

The glider flies into the thermal

The rudder attaches to the tail plane

Tail plane

IKM

A glider rides the rising air in a thermal to gain altitude.

A GLIDER'S WINGS

A glider's wings are **airfoils**, which means the wings are curved more on the top than on the bottom. When the glider moves through the air, this shape produces the force of lift.

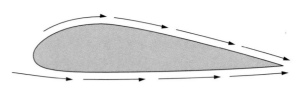

A MODERN GLIDER

Modern gliders are built of strong, but lightweight, materials. They have wide wings, a rudder on the tail, a cockpit for the pilot and a long narrow fuselage.

Today, modern gliders cruise at about 80 kilometers (50 miles) per hour but can reach 240 kilometers (149 miles) per hour in a dive. They are capable of performing nearly all of the aerobatic stunts of a powered aircraft.

Mountain ranges often create strong thermals.

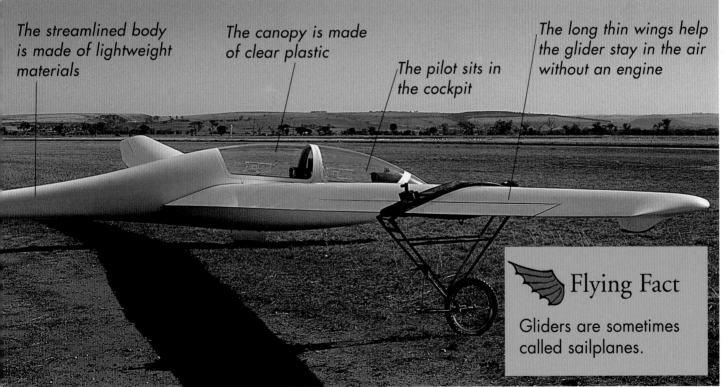

The streamlined body is made of lightweight materials

The canopy is made of clear plastic

The pilot sits in the cockpit

The long thin wings help the glider stay in the air without an engine

Flying Fact

Gliders are sometimes called sailplanes.

A glider with transportation wheels at the end of the wings.

LAUNCHING A GLIDER

Most gliders do not have an engine and need
help to take off. A glider is usually launched on a
cable attached to a winch or a powered aircraft.

A winch launch

To launch a glider with a winch, one end of a
cable is attached to the glider. The other end
is attached to a fast-revolving drum. As the
drum turns, it pulls the cable and drags the
glider into the air like a kite. As the glider
reaches the top of the steep climb, the pilot
releases the cable.

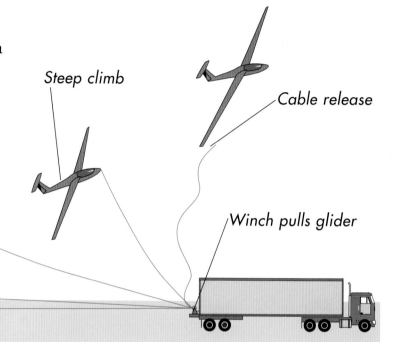

Steep climb

Cable release

Winch pulls glider

A tow launch

A tow launch is when the glider is towed behind a
light aircraft. The glider is released from the tow
cable when it has gained enough height.

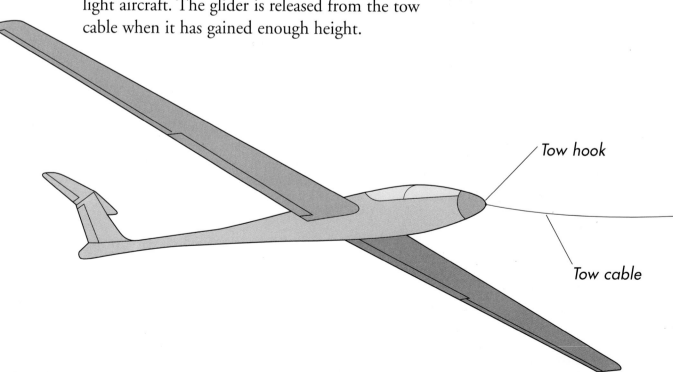

Tow hook

Tow cable

MODERN GLIDERS

Modern high-performance gliders can glide for many hours and cover hundreds of miles. They can also soar to greater heights than most propeller-driven aircraft when they are in suitable air streams.

Modern glider cockpits are so low that pilots almost lie flat on their backs as they fly. The main flight instruments of a glider are the same as for other aircraft but they do not have any fuel or engine instruments.

Airspeed indicator—shows the speed forward through the air

Altimeter—shows height

Variometer—shows the rate of climb or descent

A view from behind the pilot in a glider.

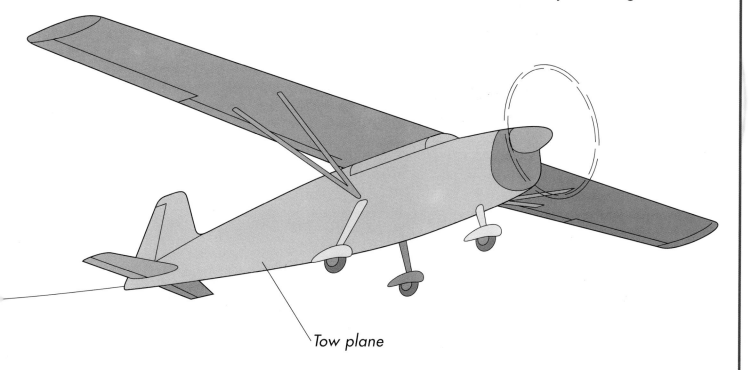

Tow plane

27

Paragliders

A PARAGLIDER IS A TYPE of glider that has developed from the parachute. It is light and compact and can be carried in a backpack. Like hang-gliders, paragliders are flown in thermals or along hillsides where the wind blows upwards.

The wing of a paraglider is made of many hollow cells of airtight fabric. The front of each cell is open to the air. Air blows into the hollow cells, inflating them and giving the wing shape. The pilot sits underneath the wing in a seat suspended by thin wires and steers from side to side.

Paragliders are based on parachute designs.

Microlights

A MICROLIGHT AIRPLANE has a simple frame like a hang-glider with an engine-driven propeller attached to it. Microlights can fly at about 65 kilometers (40 miles) per hour. Its small piston engine has the power of 40 to 60 **horsepower**.

Other microlights, known as ultra-lights, have developed into miniature aircraft with rigid wings and a trike unit. Although microlights look fragile, they are safe and reliable, as well as cheap and practical to fly.

THE TRIKE

The pilot and passenger of a flexi-wing microlight sit in the trike, or air tricycle. It has three wheels for stability when landing and taking off. The passenger sits behind and a little above the pilot. The pilot faces a control panel that has a small range of instruments including an airspeed indicator and altimeter.

Trikes in flight.

Flying Fact

Gossamer Albatross was the first pedal–powered aircraft.

Flight timeline

1783 In France brothers Joseph and Etienne Montgolfier launch the first successful hot-air balloon.

1852 The first steam-powered airship is flown by the French engineer Henri Giffard.

1890s The German engineer Otto Lilienthal builds and flies monoplane and biplane gliders.

1903 The Wright brothers make the first powered-aircraft flight at Kitty Hawk, the United States.

1909 French pilot Louis Bleriot makes the first successful airplane flight across the English Channel.

1910 The first commercial air service is established by Count Ferdinand von Zeppelin of Germany, using airships.

1914 World War I begins. Aircraft are used on both sides.

1919 Two British pilots, John Alcock and Arthur Whitten Brown, make the first non-stop flight across the Atlantic Ocean.

1927 The US pilot Charles Lindberg flies his Spirit of St. Louis solo across the Atlantic Ocean from New York to Paris.

1930 Frank Whittle of Great Britain takes out a patent for a jet engine.

1939 The first jet aircraft, the German He178, makes its first flight.

World War II begins. Aircraft are used on both sides.

American engineer Igor Sikorsky designs the first modern helicopter.

1947 Charles 'Chuck' Yeager breaks the sound barrier in the American Bell X-1 rocket plane, the first supersonic aircraft.

1952 The world's first jet airliner, the DeHavilland Comet, enters regular passenger service in the United Kingdom.

1970 The Boeing 747 jumbo jet enters service.

1975 The supersonic Concorde, the world's fastest airliner, goes into service.

1984 The X-29, the experimental plane, flies for the first time.

1986 Dick Rutan and Jeana Yeager make the first unrefuelled round-the-world flight in the Rutan Voyager.

1989 The B-2 Stealth bomber is test flown.

1999 Bernard Piccard and Brian Jones, a Swiss doctor and a British pilot, fly around the world in a hot-air balloon.

2000 and beyond New supersonic space planes may be flying around the world carrying passengers and cargo in record-breaking times.

Airships may provide regular passenger and cargo services.

The International Space Station (ISS) will be fully functional by 2004. Astronauts and scientists will commute between Earth and the ISS to live and work in space.

People may be flying between Earth and outer space as they live and work in bases on the moon and other planets.

Glossary

airfoil   the specially curved shape of an airplane wing. It produces an upward force or lift as it moves through the air

cargo   payload, such as luggage and mail goods

composite   a strong, light weight material used in aircraft construction

delta-shaped wings   triangular-shaped wings

drag   air resistance that holds back an object

elevator   the part of an aircraft that controls its angle (pitch)

glider   an aircraft that has no engine or other power source

horsepower   a measure of an engine's power

hydrogen   the lightest and most common simple substance in the universe. Hydrogen catches fire easily and was dangerous when used in airships

lift   the upward force acting on an aircraft or other flying machine that overcomes the downward force of gravity and keeps the aircraft in the air

propeller   the angled blades, shaped like a fan, that rotate to make the aircraft move forward

pylons   an extension used to support an object such as an engine or a propeller

reconnaissance   to look ahead and find out what is there

rudder   the part of an aircraft that controls whether it is turning left or right

struts   devises used to brace or give strength to a structure

thermals   the rising currents of warm air that allow gliders and birds to get lift

Index